YOUR WAY
BACK

A Course Designed to Help Moms Find and Keep the ME in Mommy

ANNE M. SMOLLON

In Mom's Corner
Be there, for yourself.

ISBN 10: 0615659276

ISBN 13: 9780615659275

To you, and your desire
to be all you can be

CONTENTS

Introduction..7

Part I: Your *Self* (Exploring who are you).........................13

Part II: Your *Values* (Identifying what you want) 65

Part III: Your *Goals* (Getting what you desire).................87

Additional Tips for Achieving Your Goal.......................105

INTRODUCTION

If you've read my book, *Missing In Action: How Mothers Lose, Grieve, and Retrieve Their Sense of Self*, you know my story. You know that I struggled immensely during the transition period that followed the birth of my first baby, and continued as my family grew to include two more children. Having read my book, you also know how love for one's child can be strong while a strange angst can deepen around feelings associated with loss, the loss of one's sense of self in the enormous responsibilities, chores, lifestyle and personal changes that seem inherent to motherhood. Within the book I cite many examples of how women typically change once they become mothers and how they often perceive an *undesirable* change as loss. I go on to describe how new moms may grieve (often unconsciously) aspects of themselves or their lives that seem "gone." As magnificent as it is to become a mom, it's hard to deny a new reality fraught with changes that relate to appearance, autonomy, sexuality, level of spousal intimacy, sleeping habits, energy, friendships, career goals and ambitions, self-esteem, and financial independence. It's even harder still to deny the fact that these changes can, and often do, impact the integrity of one's "self."

If you've read *Missing In Action*, you know that I coined the term Maternal Intrapersonal Anxiety (MIA) to reflect the manifestation of unrecognized and unacknowledged grief when moms lose their sense of identity—their sense of self—as the undesirable changes go unaddressed and the demands, sacrifices, and responsibilities of motherhood expand. By using the term

MIA, women can more easily describe what's going on for them and can share their feelings without fumbling over a lengthy explanation. It was my earnest desire to bring this silent epidemic to the forefront of conversation so that no mother feels alone. For many moms, the adjustment to mother-hood is a bumpy road, full of twists and turns up, down, and around major challenges that are rarely discussed. I wanted to change that through my writing of *Missing In Action*.

And finally, if you've read my book, you understand more clearly how personal boundaries can fall apart when women have children and how weak boundaries slowly destroy the core values that are central to a healthy sense of self. If you've read *Missing In Action*, you've contem-plated the questions I pose in Chapter 6, and you've pursued the goals I suggest in Chapters 7 and 8 to find your "self." Throughout the book, I know I've made clear that we are good, caring, and loving moms despite the personal angst and "growing pains" we experience ourselves as we as-pire to fit the role and become the best moms we can be for our children.

What I may not have made clear, though, is what I believe is the most *direct* path moms can take to strengthen and secure their sense of self. This direct path takes moms from the changes that occurred since they became moms and toward the core values that give meaning to their lives and spark the personal ambitions, talents, and goals that empower them to be their best selves. **Pursuing a personal interest, talent, or ambition serves as the best, most effective self-care tool available to moms.** By pursuing your personal interests/talents/ambitions, you fill the proverbial well so that the well never runs dry. Rather, it remains full and robust to serve you and those you love in the best possible ways. I discovered this (my ah-ha moment) when I started to design my new web site exclusively for moms called In Mom's Corner. While I was networking, drafting content, designing a logo, and composing my mission statement, I realized that I never felt better! I had lots of energy, especially when I was talking about In Mom's Corner. I was excited about life and the endeavor at hand. I felt happy, confident, familiar to myself, and able to give to my family without the push and pull that I had experienced in the past. I was clearly a different (and better) person and mom when I was engaging something that really mattered to *me*. Huh. I put "me" into mommy!

So, the goal of this workbook is to help do the same for you, if you're ready to take care of yourself in the most exciting, rewarding, and effective way I know. This workbook will help you explore your "self" and your life as it is now (Part 1), the core values that give meaning to your life in substantial ways (Part 2), and the path that leads you toward incorporating those values into the talents, interests, and goals that feed you and lift your mood, energy, and outlook on life (Part 3). This workbook (and the support found at www.InMomsCorner.com) will serve as a great self-care tool as you seek to be the best version of yourself. As you progress through this workbook, you will sense the effect taking hold. By the time you finish, you will see yourself as you are *now*, know what matters most to you, and be ready to embrace the personal ambitions, talents, hobbies, and/or goals that will empower you and lift you beyond the craziness and exhaustion that comes with having children (what we lovingly refer to as motherhood). There *is* a place for *you* while you mother your children. It's not *all* about them. They need you, but you must have your needs met, too. **Remember, you are fueled by the energy stored in your personal interests and ambitions.** The good news is that when you take care of yourself in this way, you have more to give to your family. So, in actuality, you're doing this for you *and* for them (which makes you feel good, I know).

Since we all learn in different ways and at different speeds, pace yourself accordingly and keep moving, even if you can't answer some of the questions. I've asked a lot of questions because journaling in itself is very cathartic and often a way of exposing some feelings, concerns, and insights we would never have realized otherwise. Journaling, and answering a variety of questions in different ways, leads to clarity. If you have trouble answering any of the questions, don't worry. Hopefully, by the end of the workbook, you will be able to go back and fill in the questions that originally stumped you. Whether you struggle through this workbook or breeze through it, be proud of yourself for engaging this process and the challenge to become more in charge of your life. Keep this workbook handy and refer to it often, as it's a guide when you temporarily lose your way or when you decide to pursue another goal. This is a keepsake for sure. It'll be fun to look at long after you've raised your kids and moved into a different phase of life. This workbook could also be a fun thing to share with your daughter(s) if/when they become mothers themselves!

For the time being, though, this workbook is intended to be for, and about, *you*. Do your very best at providing answers that reflect you and your relationship to the world. I urge you to be as honest as possible when answering these questions and find a safe place to put this workbook so that your privacy is preserved, should this be an issue for you. When you're done, I'm hoping you'll have a better sense of who you are, what's important to you, and how to live into your greatest personal ambitions because this path will never fail to give you joy and energy as you take on the "hardest job in the world" (a la Oprah). Enjoy the process and the strong, vibrant, and healthy sense of self you're developing along the way!

On a final note, I want to thank you for allowing me to join you on this journey. I have worked hard in my own life to find and secure my sense of self, and I've worked even harder figuring out how to stay ahead of the sabotaging forces at play and to pursue my goals even though the call to motherhood rings as loud as ever. This workbook reflects that hard work and will no doubt be a challenge for you to get through; however, it's a challenge worth taking, trust me. When you know who you are and have a strong sense of self, you handle life with children with greater poise, pleasure, and space for yourself. You are less likely to be swallowed up by motherhood and left depleted.

I know what that feels like. But those days are long gone, and today, I look at my children and am so proud of the young adults they've become and the relationships I've developed with them. I believe I have these wonderful relationships (my teenagers still like hanging out with me!) because I learned to give to myself; I learned how to take care of myself in ways that allowed me to be more available and attentive to them. I learned *how* to be self-centered—as in keeping my "self" centered. There's a reason why the flight attendant instructs the adult to put on the air mask first before assisting minors when there's turbulence during the flight. We can't possibly care for our children if we're struggling for air ourselves. InMomsCorner.com and this workbook are devoted to helping you find your "self" and the "oxygen" you need to live *your* best life so that you thrive—personally and in your role as mom. This workbook is an exercise that's good for you, and ultimately, good for them.

PART 1
Your *Self*

o o o o o o o o o o o o o o o o o o o o o o o o o o o o o

"Drastic change creates an estrangement from the self, and generates a need for a new birth of a new identity. And it perhaps depends on the way this need is satisfied whether the process of change runs smoothly or is attended with convulsions and explosions."

—*Eric Hoffer, The Temper of Our Time*

With Hoffer's quote in mind, I willingly admit that the "drastic change" that accompanied my transition into motherhood caused an estrangement from my "self," "convulsions and explosions," and the "need for a new birth of a new identity." Obviously, this defining moment in my life, did NOT run smoothly for me. As utterly breathtaking as it was to give birth, and as devoted as any mom could be, I also remember how quickly I began to blur in the haze of early motherhood. Lack of sleep certainly didn't help, but even as I found sleep, the haze seemed to get thicker, and before long, I couldn't recognize the once familiar face staring back at me in the bathroom mirror. So, no judgment here, as you begin this workbook by filling in the ways in which you changed since becoming a mom. As I noted in *Missing In Action*, all women change once they become mothers. This is indisputable.

Women experience changes in their physique, almost immediately, with waistlines that expand and breasts that enlarge. However, over time, other changes occur, changes in mood, friendships, level of spousal intimacy, autonomy, income potential, daily routines, priorities, and self—esteem (to name a few). It's important to look closely at the changes you experienced because with each change may have come a sense of loss. If the loss is perceived as significant, you may have—or still need—to grieve that loss, and grieve it without criticism, judgment, or guilt. I wholeheartedly believe that this process of letting go of life as it was before kids needs to happen so that you can grab hold of all that life can be after kids—a life that *includes* what's important to you personally (e.g., seeing friends, working out, going back to school, career, hobbies). It's also important to acknowledge how you've changed... because you *have* changed. I want you to literally see on paper how you (and your lifestyle) changed because you have new pieces/elements/circumstances/priorities to consider as you move forward to create a new identity and the life you want to live. So, we begin with the changes you've experienced since becoming a mom.

The most obvious changes are likely related to your physical appearance. Below, describe how your body changed *after* the initial onslaught of changes that pregnancy creates. For instance, many women lose much of the true "baby weight" that they gained over nine months, but a significant number of women struggle to recover their pre-pregnancy jean size or reach a weight that feels ideal.

Changes in physique (e.g., weight gain, breast size, foot size, hair, complexion, stubborn stretch marks). Describe the changes below.

little change_____   noticeable change_____   significant change_____

_____

_____

_____

_____

I've had several moms ask me if I could research whether or not illness among women increased after motherhood. It sounded like an interesting project, but I never took it on. However, I do know from my many speaking engagements that women tend to experience a decline in their health once they have children. I'm not sure if this is about age, stress, or other circumstances (e.g., marital/economic status, cultural background), but it is what it is. Personally, I ran into Graves' Disease (hyperactive thyroid) shortly after I had Daniel, my third (and last). This is an auto-immune disease that's related to stress, according to my doctor. This doctor also wanted to "destroy" my thyroid and prescribe meds to replace what was destroyed. I was days away from allowing him to "treat" me when I broke down in tears while talking to my mother. I didn't want to go through with a procedure that would fill my thyroid with so much radiation that my doctor suggested I check into a hotel for a couple of days so my children wouldn't be exposed. Can you imagine?! Right then and there, in tears, I vowed to keep my thyroid and stop the stress. I vowed to get my life back and to avoid those things and people that created undue stress in me. I vowed to *figure it out* (create boundaries, build my self-esteem, etc.)... and I did. A year and a half later (with my thyroid in place), a blood test revealed that my thyroid levels were normal.

Changes in physical health (e.g., headaches, body aches, any illnesses related to your auto-immune system or symptoms related to stress, low energy, sleep issues/ fatigue, heart palpitations, asthma). Jot down your experience.

little change_____ noticeable change_____ significant change_____

_____

_____

_____

_____

_____

_____

If you need to see the pictures, I'll gladly show them. I was a visual nightmare. What the heck happened to me?! My dress code demanded flats, room to move, and permanent stains. I was afraid to color my gray hair for fear of the chemicals affecting any future pregnancies. I wore my maternity clothes even *after* giving birth. Why? I don't know. I guess I was thinking, "Why not?" I didn't think much about what to wear—I had no time to think. I know it may never have happened this way, but I have a memory of myself walking through the mall with my double stroller and thinking that people were looking at me—not the cute kids in the stroller. And, I knew what they were thinking. "Poor mommy. She needs a makeover!"

Changes in appearance (e.g., clothing/dress code, overall appearance, hair and hygiene issues)

little change_____   noticeable change_____   significant change_____

Be honest. No one else has to see this.

How about changes in your mood? I noticed over the first few years of motherhood that I lost my sense of humor. I mean, I still laughed at funny things, but I didn't generate the humor as I used to do. I think I became a little less (ok, a lot less) fun. I remember thinking that I was probably just tired and overwhelmed. I guess I was tired and overwhelmed a lot.

Changes in mood (e.g., more emotional, less patience, mood swings, irritability)

little change_____   noticeable change_____   significant change_____

It might be useful to ask someone else what he/she has noticed, although this may sting a little. You could ask questions such as "Do I strike you as less patient than I was before being a mom?" "Do I seem depressed / irritable /uptight?" "Do I seem different to you since I had [your child's name]?" Just listen (don't debate) and know you're on your way to creating the balance in your life that will work for you and help you be all that you want to be. Jot down your thoughts on this.

_____

_____

_____

_____

_____

_____

I know for many women, friendships change in early motherhood, especially if your friends are not having babies. If they are having babies, they are just as busy and consumed as you. Hopefully, though, you will eventually be traveling down the same roads, so to speak, and be able to maintain your friendships to some degree. However, if your friends are not having babies, it will be more difficult to keep in touch. My best friend and I went our own ways. Neither of us planned for this to happen, and I can hardly believe that it did. But, I understand how it happened. She was single and continued to travel a lot like I had done before my first baby. Teresa would call and visit occasionally, but those calls and visits became less and less frequent. She knew I couldn't always take her call, and I knew she couldn't possibly understand. We are friends to this day, even though we have very different lives and don't see each other often. The good news is that I developed new friendships with women who were in my stage of life—on the verge of starting families. One friend in particular (Danya) remains my closest friend to this day.

I can't imagine my life without her. As I wrote in the Acknowledgments of *Missing In Action*, she redefined my concept of friendship.

Changes in friendships (e.g., amount of time spent with friends, topics of conversation, old friends vs. new friends)

little change _____   noticeable change_____   significant change_____

Describe how this feels.

_____

_____

_____

_____

_____

Let's talk *sex*. How has *that* been between you and your partner? How would your husband/partner answer that question? For most couples, sex is a challenge once baby comes along. Time, fatigue, and lack of interest top the list of excuses. It was all three for me. This can certainly stress a marriage. And, men, although wanting to understand, can't fully understand what we're going through and all we've got going on (i.e., adjusting to all the changes in our lives and body). Generally speaking, I think men want life (aka sex life) to resume as it was prior to children as quickly as possible. I don't remember ever hearing a new mom say this.

Changes in spousal/primary relationship: intimacy (e.g., less physical contact, such as handholding, kissing, love making; your level of desire)

little change_____   noticeable change_____   significant change_____

You may want to ask your husband/partner what he/she has noticed. The feedback may likely spark a dialogue. Be prepared.

_____

_____

_____

_____

_____

_____

Although our sex life suffered, my husband and I managed to keep our relationship intact. Fortunately I do have an understanding husband. He realized the great shift that had taken place in my life (more than his) and supported me every step of the way. Believe me, we went through our ups and downs, but love prevailed. It takes effective communication, support, understanding, and compromise, for sure.

Changes in spousal/primary relationship in general (e.g., amount of arguments, quality time spent together, emotional availability—either yours or his, method and tone of communication, thoughtful gestures)

little change_____   noticeable change_____   significant change_____

Cite some examples.

_____

_____

_____

At twenty-one years old, I was self-sufficient. I worked, paid my bills, and enjoyed a comfortable living. At the time I conceived (I was 34), I was making a very good living in Research & Development at a standardized testing company. I expected to go back to work after Leigh Ann was born, but she had a brain hemorrhage at birth, which led me to change my plans. I never did go back. Leigh Ann needed more care than the average baby, and then, Laura was soon on the way (perhaps I should have given *this* plan a little more thought). The years slipped by. I worked to keep up the house and take care of the children, and my husband worked. We agreed to this plan. However, I was financially dependent on my husband, and that took some getting used to. He was happy to provide, but it always felt odd not having my own income stream.

Changes in financial status (i.e., Have you maintained financial independence or did you become financially dependent on your spouse once the baby came, or have things remained the same?)

little change_____   noticeable change_____   significant change_____

Describe how this makes you feel.

_____

_____

_____

_____

_____

_____

Oh boy. This one is another biggie. Changes in your lifestyle. I've got to believe there will be a few on this list, at least. Certainly my sleeping habits changed. I always loved going to bed late and sleeping in...late. I used to go to the gym twice a day. Between the stair stepper and the pool, I was good. I enjoyed hanging out with friends at the gym, having a snack at the snack bar, and then out to do whatever I was in the mood to do. Usually this meant a trip down to the beach (I lived on Long Island prior to marriage and kids). My friend, Teresa, would meet me there, often times with food and wine. I was the quintessential bachelorette. No real schedule, no great priorities, and no routine apart from my workouts. You can see how motherhood took me by storm!

Changes in lifestyle (e.g., schedule, priorities/obligations, daily routines)

little change_____   noticeable change_____   significant change_____

I know you have something to say here.

I vividly remember the day I submitted my application to the Rutgers Graduate School of Social Work and what I said to my husband at the time, which was "I'll either get accepted or start a family." I honestly didn't think I would get accepted. I applied half-heartedly. The application required a statement outlining my reasons for applying. I drifted so far from their mission statement that I never thought they'd consider me. And statistics were not in my favor, as the school had a very high rejection rate. In other words, I was (subconsciously) planning a family. I'm sure you know how this ends. Yes, I was accepted, and I had a big decision to make. I'm all about having choices, and so, with this degree, I knew I would be creating more choices for myself. So, I started my MSW program. *And*, soon after, I conceived. I stayed in school until I delivered. It was years before I went back to finish what I had started.

Changes in personal goals (e.g., finish school, complete a project, pursue a career, learn a skill)

little change_____   noticeable change_____   significant change_____

Describe how this feels.

_____

_____

_____

_____

_____

_____

_____

_____

Considering the fact that I didn't have much of a daily schedule prior to kids, there were *many* changes to my daily schedule after kids. The biggest change was that I *had* a schedule, as chaotic as it was. I mean I didn't *really* have a schedule when babies started coming along. I kind of "wung" it. But, the daily routine always included things I had never done before, such as nursing, changing diapers, doing lots of laundry, watching *Barney*, strolling aimlessly around the backyard, neighborhood, and "plaza" down the street. Once I filled the day with the odds and ends that are certain to delight a child (playgrounds, picnics and the like), I finished up each day with the standard closing of dinner, bath, story time, and bed. Toss in laundry day, cleaning, and food shopping, and my weekly schedule was complete.

Changes in daily schedule (vs. what you were doing prior to baby)

little change_____   noticeable change_____   significant change_____

_____

_____

_____

_____

_____

_____

_____

_____

Your living space is another interesting area to explore because our homes are supposed to be our sanctuaries, the place to escape the craziness of the world, a place to rejuvenate, a place that reflects the general nature of our being. Our home is our safe haven where we can be who we are and where we can express our individuality. Having a baby in the home does change the "flavor" of that space. How do you feel about that? When you are home, are you surrounded by comforting things, including sounds, colors, lighting, and all the simple pleasures related to home? Do you see reflections of your "self" in your home? I don't recall (years ago) seeing much in our house that reflected who I was. I do remember buying an easel, thinking that one day I would refine the skills necessary to create a decent painting (the easel is still in my closet). My writing books had long been put away, and I almost never sat at my desk with pen in hand—the desk had become a landing station for bottles, toys, and my diaper bag. I should have known then that I was in trouble. I recognize now that our mood, self-image, energy, and outlook on life are shaped in great part by our surroundings and what we expose ourselves to each and every day.

Changes in your living space/your home (e.g., noise, clutter, people, furniture, colors, light, evidence of you)

Little change_____ noticeable change_____ significant change_____

Oh yes, another biggie for me. My self-image; it plummeted. Eek. Prior to kids, I had always felt good about myself. I was nice-looking, very personable/likeable, fit, funny, and smart. Not a 10 on any one of these scales, but all together, not bad. I liked myself. That's always a good sign, and reflective of a good self-image. So, what happened? Well, that's a good question. I'll tell you what I suppose. I suppose I didn't adjust well to being a mother. There was so much to handle, so much to figure out, so much to do. Given that my husband worked, I was home alone to take full responsibility of this small, dependent creature. Her life was in my hands. Oh my! Everything else went by the wayside, and I didn't care. At the time, I didn't care that my hair was turning gray or my clothes had stains all over them. I didn't care that our apartment was messy or that I didn't shower for days. But slowly, and surreptitiously, not caring took my self-image hostage.

Changes in self-image (i.e., Do you see yourself as less desirable or less interesting; that is, less of whatever you felt good about prior to motherhood?)

little change_____   noticeable change_____   significant change_____

Describe this change and how it makes you feel.

_____

_____

_____

_____

_____

_____

_____

I was too young to be forgetting so much. Oh, that's right. I became a mom, and I was on overload; exhausted and lost in the chaos of motherhood. Despite all the advice I got on how to make lists so that I could keep up, I rarely kept up and the lists didn't work. My brain could only handle so much, and then it would stop. I would forget things, lose things, or worse... slip during conversations and use words like "super-deedooper." How embarrassing, especially when in the company of academics and former co-workers.

Changes in cognitive skills/brain power (e.g., difficulty concentrating, keeping a thought, or remembering things)

little change_____   noticeable change_____   significant change_____

Cite an example of this change in brain power. It will be fun to look back and reread someday!

_____

_____

_____

I was never that into big gatherings or seeing lots of friends all at once. I'm a very one-on-one kind of gal with the good friends I have. Unfortunately, more often than not, my one-on-one time became more like two-on-one or two-on-two and then three-on-two, four-on-three, etc. You get it. Children outnumbered us adults. And the social time became a "play date" where my girlfriend and I *might* get to finish a conversation, if we were lucky. Looking back, it's endearing, but then, not so much, especially when you're desperate for adult time. You can tweet and facebook all you want, but nothing can replace face-to-face quality time with a close friend—nothing!

Changes in social calendar (i.e., adult gatherings, friends' night out)

little change_____   noticeable change_____   significant change_____

_____

_____

_____

_____

_____

_____

No question, I felt trapped more than once. It's hard to admit, but admitting it is necessary in order to move into a better place. When a mom says she feels trapped, people conclude pretty instantly that she resents ever having children. This is not true. Even when I felt my worst, I smiled knowing I had my children. I just couldn't figure out how to balance life in a way that included me and what I thought was important for my well-being and personal growth and development... because those things were important to me too.

Note: If this section resonates with you to any great degree, please consider reading my book, *Missing In Action: How Mothers Lose, Grieve, and Retrieve Their Sense of Self.* For more information about the content in my book, please visit www.inmomscorner.com.

Changes in emotional well-being (i.e., Do you feel isolated or "trapped"? Do you feel alone in your experience? Do you battle depression, feel fragile or feel as though you're living on the edge?)

little change_____   noticeable change_____   significant change_____

_____

_____

_____

_____

_____

Negative self-talk will take you down. What we say to ourselves definitely impacts our actions and self-esteem. Many of us repeat the same expressions, the same condescending, disparaging words over and over again. "I just can't do this anymore." Or, "What's the matter with me?" Or, "I can't do anything right." Yuck. But, I was as guilty of doing this as anyone. I still catch myself doing it. Over the last several years, as I was preparing *Missing In Action*, this companion workbook, my ebooks, worksheets, and my In Mom's Corner blog, I had a nasty tendency to say things like "You're not going to get this done." "You can't do this." I think I would have gotten to this point in my career and in my business a lot sooner had I not used these kinds of negative statements. As a practitioner of Neuro-Linguistic Programming (NLP), I know better. NLP is the study of human perception as it relates to communication (including interpersonal, self-talk, and body language) and its impact on behavior. I know our self-talk directs us toward success or failure, happiness or misery, sickness and health. Thank goodness I began to "check" my internal dialogue, stop the negative talk, and build my self-esteem step-by-step with the kind of work you're doing now.

For more information about how words influence our behavior and how you can reframe your negative self-talk, please register at www.inmomscorner.com where you can join our discussions, read blog posts, and enroll in group activities around this topic.

Changes in your internal dialogue; that is, what you say to yourself (i.e., Do you feel different/bad and tell yourself so? Do you talk to yourself in a negative tone or with negative content?)

Little change_____   noticeable change_____   significant change_____

What negative statements do you constantly repeat in your head?

_____

_____

_____

_____

_____

I don't think many things feel quite as bad as looking into a mirror and not recognizing the person you see standing there. That's usually a bad day, but quite common among moms. I can refer you to several TV shows or movies that have referenced this feeling in one or more episodes. *Desperate Housewives* comes to mind immediately, although shows such as *Sex and the City* and *Brothers and Sisters* have brought up this topic as well as movies, including Marley & Me with Jennifer Aniston. This phenomenon appears to be an inherent element of motherhood. I lost my sense of self, like most moms, which is why I was determined to take a closer look at the underlying dynamics, interview lots of moms, record my findings, and expound on my theory for it. Hence, my book, *Missing In Action*. It's a topic very close to my heart, and a topic I truly believe needs to be addressed so that mothers thrive as women on a fulfilling and rewarding journey through motherhood with their "self" intact.

Changes in overall sense of self (i.e., Do you recognize yourself when you look in the mirror? Do you feel like you're buried under the heavy load of motherhood? Do you look different, sound different, or act different?

Do you have trouble identifying the things that you need, want, and prefer in life? Do you know who you are apart from "mom" and the other roles you play? Do you feel lost? Have you lost a certain degree of confidence or self-esteem?)

Little change_____   noticeable change_____   significant change_____

Tell me about this in detail. This is a critical component of the workbook, and I have a feeling you'll come back to this section often.

_____

_____

_____

_____

_____

_____

_____

_____

_____

_____

_____

Now that we've explored several ways in which you or your lifestyle may have changed, take a minute to compose a Miss List. In the column on the left, jot down ten things you miss since you became a mom. In the column on the right, pick five of those ten things that you want back in your life as soon as possible.

Things I Miss   Things I want back

1.   1.
2.   2.
3.   3.
4.   4.
5.   5.
6.
7.
8.
9.
10.

Considering this list, have you ever caught yourself using the word "lost" to describe how things changed in your life since becoming a mom? For example, "I lost my freedom." Or, "I lost my desire for sex." Or, "I lost touch with several of my friends." Or, "I feel like I'm losing control of my life." I mention this because often women perceive change in their lives as loss, and they actually *use* the word "lost" when discussing it. When we lose something of value and go beyond simply missing it, we're likely to experience a sense of grief. Grief can find its way to us in many different ways, from big ways to small ways—it manifests itself in physical, psychological, social, and cognitive ways. Below is a list of symptoms related to grief that I composed for my book (from the most obvious to the most obscure). I found it striking that the mothers I interviewed had so many symptoms that paralleled the classic symptoms of grief.

Physical Symptoms

- fatigue, restlessness/overactivity
- stress-related illnesses (e.g., thyroid disease/Graves' disease, MS, ir-ritable bowel syndrome)
- a general decline in health (stomach/intestinal problems, high blood pressure, asthma, GERD)
- sleeping problems (e.g., night waking, insomnia)
- muscle tension (headaches, backaches, etc.)
- tightness in the throat or chest
- decrease or increase of appetite (weight loss/gain)
- low energy, palpitations, oversensitivity to noise

Emotional/Psychological Symptoms

- irritability/lowered tolerance, anger
- depression, anxiety
- sadness (e.g., abrupt or prolonged bouts of crying)
- loss of identity, sudden changes in mood (mood swings), self-doubt
- irrational fears, self-consciousness
- decreased self-esteem
- lack of self-concern
- a feeling of losing one's mind
- preoccupation with a former reality
- denial, regression, and other defense mechanisms
- guilt/shame, resentment
- a sense of failure or fear of failure
- despair, feelings of helplessness

Cognitive Symptoms

- absentmindedness, difficulty concentrating or remembering
- disorganization (e.g., starting one task and leaving it unfinished to start another task)
- impaired decision-making and intellectual processing
- negative internal dialogue (self-talk)
- distorted perceptions of self and others

Social/Behavioral Symptoms

- withdrawal/avoidance of others, loneliness, isolation
- withdrawal from normal activity or activities that previously held great interest
- a strain in relationships
- sexual difficulties (e.g., performance, desire, and intimacy)
- increased use of nicotine, alcohol, or other drugs
- chemical addiction relapse
- excessive use of television as a means of escaping
- difficulty having fun with family or friends
- the interruption of usual patterns of behavior

I have always believed that it's important to recognize (and reconcile with) any grief attached to an element of your life or self that you perceive as "lost." Since most of these symptoms are self-explanatory, you need only to assess whether or not you see parallels between these symptoms and how you feel, act, and think. Unrecognized and unacknowledged grief may lead to Maternal Intrapersonal Anxiety (MIA), as described in my book, *Missing In Action*, and may sabotage any efforts you make in finding and securing your sense of self. MIA *is* the manifestation of unrecognized and unacknowledged grief when women lose their pre-child identity as the demands, sacrifices, and responsibilities of motherhood increase.

Perceived loss of physical appearance, personality traits (e.g., sense of humor, easy-going nature), sexuality, financial status (personal income or income potential), prior lifestyle, relationships, personal goals and ambitions (e.g., career), self-esteem, etc. impact the integrity of mom's "self" because these are typically *valued* aspects of her life, identity, and experience of womanhood in general. Losing something of value, whether it's a person, place, object, image, idea, or construct (e.g., sense of self), generates grief. Therefore, a threat to the integrity of mom's "self" can cause anxiety, a sort of separation anxiety (from self) that leads to the symptoms resembling grief. Moms often know and describe this feeling but rarely, if ever, recognize or acknowledge it as grief. Please refer to my book *Missing In Action: How Mothers Lose, Grieve, and Retrieve Their Sense of Self* for a more in-depth discussion of MIA and its impact on women and their sense of self.

Moving on, in this next list, I want you to jot down twelve things that define you. They can be random words of things you love (e.g. the color green, tennis, violin, ice cream, traveling, knitting) or people you love, or a role you play in life (e.g., teacher, artist, comedian, disciplinarian, provider). They can be adjectives, adverbs, or nouns. They can be words that you have not yet been able to *fully* realize but always wished for the chance. I ask that you remove all self-imposing limits and let the words flow as effortlessly as possible. Make this fun.

1. _____

2. _____

3. _____

4. _____

5. _____

6. _____

7. _____

8. _____

9. _____

10. _____

11. _____

12. _____

Now that you see, and literally feel the certainty of, each definable aspect of *you*, rewrite the list in the order of that certainty and degree of ownership. In other words, pick and choose each thing according to how close it is to your true self—number 1 being the closest and number 12 being the farthest on this list. I don't suppose this exercise will be easy; it's meant to push you toward self-discovery and self-awareness, and highlight how you can best express your "self."

"Words are a form of action, capable of influencing change." Ingrid Bengis

1. _____

2. _____

3. _____

4. _____

5. _____

6. _____

7. _____

8. _____

9. _____

10. _____

11. _____

12. _____

In doing this exercise, you take ownership of the words you write. Of course, during different times of your life, the words you pick may be different than the words you're choosing today. The point is that you're living in the NOW, and I want to help you move closer to "being" each word that you relate to NOW, in your quest to find, build, and secure your sense of self. If you choose a word that's not feasible in your new life as mom, let it go. And I mean if it's truly not possible to incorporate now. In the course of our lives, we will enter into and leave many "chapters." Our story consists of infancy, toddlerhood, childhood, tween, teen, young adult, adult, etc. and each chapter has its own distinct voice, characters, and elements. Time makes it impossible to stay long in any one chapter, and eventually we must say goodbye. As written in Judith Viorst's best-selling book, *Necessary Losses*, we experience loss throughout our lifetime. The trick is to live in the present, recognize ourselves in each chapter, accept the opportunities that are presented to us at each phase of life, and prepare the way for the dreams, goals, and ambitions that dangle in our future.

If you wrote down a word that you cannot live into because circumstances prohibit it, you may want to scratch this off the list because it will only frustrate you to pursue something you can't have right now. Perhaps this desire will come to fruition during a different chapter of your life, a time that allows you to bask in its glory. For now, you do have a family to include into your life and plans; however, a family shouldn't prevent you from being true to your "self."

As moms, we "have to" do many things. I get this, but I also get that if I don't take care of myself in the most effective and fundamental ways, I can feel depleted, lost, and disconnected with my "self" rather quickly, which creates mounds of "bad" feelings shortly thereafter. None of this feels good.

Yes, there's a lot to do. This is true, but you have to add your "self" to that list of things to do. Make it a habit, and you'll get through all those other "have to" things a lot easier. When you nourish your "self," you give to others what *is* there to give. So ask yourself what there is to give when you're feeling as though the well is running dry (or is dry). Not the best of you, that's for sure. I can remember saying to myself, "I'm functioning at burnout." This is not sustainable or healthy. The bottom line is that there's no way a well fills itself. You must fill it, and fill it with the activities and people that give you energy, lift your spirits, and define the "self" you most want to be.

Do you want to draw a picture of your "self" as you want it? Try it. At worst, you'll get a great laugh. At best, you'll create a vision of possibilities. The more detail, the more color, and the more dimension, the better. Or, let your creative juices flow by designing a symbol that represents and incorporates what you value or seek. Refer to this drawing often as you move through this workbook and during the months ahead. Some women have found this exercise worth doing because they were literally able to *see* what they wanted to create.

Next I'm going to ask you a series of questions, random questions. From there we will look to focus in on your core values. As defined in my material, a value is something we deem as significant and meaningful in our lives. Core values reflect the beliefs, feelings, needs, hopes, thoughts, desires, and experiences that make up our "personal profile." While interviewing moms, I unearthed many values, such as friendship, self-respect, appearance, power, achievement, wisdom, compassion, spirituality, personal development, security, confidence, loyalty, and adventure. However, this is just a sample of the values that one can embrace. We'll look into your values, but first answer these questions, so we can get the most complete snapshot of your life right now.

How physically healthy are you?
Great health_____ Good health_____ Poor health_____
Explain in more detail.

_____

_____

_____

_____

_____

How mentally healthy are you?
Great health_____Good health_____ Poor health_____
Elaborate on this.

_____

_____

_____

_____

_____

Do you get enough sleep?
Plenty_____ Decent_____ Not nearly enough_____

Do you take a sleep aid?   Yes_____ No_____

How much sleep do you think would be best for you?

_____

What prevents you from getting this amount of sleep?

_____

_____

Do you generally get along well with your spouse?
Very well_____ Good_____Fair_____Bad_____
Explain.

_____

_____

_____

_____

Do you believe your spouse will support you finding and securing your "self"?
Absolutely_____ I think so_____ Maybe_____ No_____
How does this make you feel?

_____

_____

_____

_____

How would your spouse describe you on a good day?

_____

_____

_____

_____

Are your friends supportive of your needs and ambitions?
Absolutely_____ I think so_____ Maybe_____ No _____

Tell me about your friends.

_____

_____

_____

_____

Do your friends know that you're struggling in your role as mom?
Absolutely, because I've told them_____
I think so, because I show signs and symptoms of distress_____
Maybe, because I do a good job at hiding my feelings and problems_____
No, because I avoid my friends or never bring up the topic_____

Provide three words that your best friend would use to describe you.

_____

_____

_____

Does your family of origin (e.g., mother, father, siblings) support you and your desire to live your best life?

Absolutely_____ I think so_____ Maybe_____ No_____

Our sibling(s) and parents can be a tricky topic of conversation. Generally speaking, many of us have dysfunctional families, to one degree or an-other. Tell me a little bit about your family of origin and your role in that family as it was and the way it is now.

_____

_____

_____

_____

_____

What do you like most about your life?

_____

_____

_____

_____

What do you like least about your life right now?

_____

_____

_____

_____

What do you like most about yourself?

_____

_____

_____

What do you like least about yourself?

_____

_____

_____

_____

List five personal strengths.

_____

_____

_____

_____

_____

List five personal weaknesses.

_____

_____

_____

_____

_____

Tell me whether or not you think those weaknesses can sabotage your achievement of any personal goals you set for yourself in the months to come. For instance, one weakness of mine is time management, which I knew I had to conquer if I wanted to create a successful business.

_____

_____

_____

_____

_____

How well do you get along with your children?
Really well_____ Pretty good_____ Good_____ Not good_____
Note the ages of your children and explain your answer.

_____

_____

_____

_____

_____

Do you think by improving your self-image/self-esteem and strengthening your sense of self, you can improve the family dynamics in your home and the relationship(s) you have with your child(ren)?

Absolutely_____ Probably_____ Maybe_____ No_____
Explain your answer.

_____

_____

_____

_____

Do you tend to be an optimist_____ or a pessimist_____

Describe a typical conversation you have with yourself whether you describe yourself as an optimist or a pessimist. In other words, what kind of things do you tell yourself on a regular basis about the relationships, circumstances, and events in your life?

_____

_____

_____

_____

_____

What makes you angry?

_____

_____

_____

What is your greatest source of stress?

_____

_____

_____

List five sources of comfort.

For me, fleece pajamas, a good cup of coffee, a facial, a hug, and the sound of the ocean come instantly to my mind.

_____

_____

_____

_____

_____

How would you describe the general tone in your home?
(e.g., pleasant, crazy, loud, tense, fun, hostile, easy)

Explain and highlight what you either like or don't like about this tone.

_____

_____

_____

_____

Where do you go when you need a break?

_____

What do you do when you need a break?

_____

What's your favorite season and why?

_____

_____

_____

Have you developed a personal philosophy for your life?
Tell me about it.

_____

_____

_____

Are you living in harmony with your philosophy (most of the time)?
Yes_____   No_____
If no, what would you say creates the conflict?

_____

_____

_____

If no, what would help you be aligned with your personal philosophy?

_____

_____

_____

Do you believe in an energy force greater than yourself; that is, a higher being, such as God or a spiritual reality beyond yourself?

Yes_____   No_____

If yes, how does this spiritual aspect of yourself get fulfilled and/or affect your well-being? How does this presence in your life manifest itself?

_____

_____

_____

_____

What do you want that you don't have? This could be anything (e.g., money, fame, peace of mind, time, faith, a nice car). What comes to mind?

_____

_____

If you like to read (and have time to read), do you read to learn (non-fiction) or to escape (fiction)?

_____

_____

List three role models; people you admire or aspire to be like.

_____

_____

_____

Tell me why you admire these people.

_____

_____

_____

_____

The greatest compliment you ever received was

when_____

_____

_____

What inspires you? (e.g., money, acknowledgment, personal satisfaction, art)

_____

_____

What do you want to be doing in your life right now that you're not doing? Why is this important to you?

_____

_____

_____

_____

Do you tend to blame others for what you are not achieving in life?
Yes_____ No_____
If yes, who do you blame?

_____

_____

How have you overcome bouts of sadness or depression in the past?

_____

_____

_____

Do you tend to be inherently motivated or do you need others to motivate you?
Intrinsic/inwardly motivated_____   Extrinsic/externally motivated_____

What "gifts" do you willingly and happily share with others? For example, you might be a good listener, or you're compassionate, or you know how to food shop for a family of five for less than $10 (as per The Frugal Family).

Describe your gifts.

_____

_____

_____

Do you care about what you think and feel to be true of yourself more than what others may think and believe about you? In other words, how affected are you by the opinions of others? Explain.

_____

_____

_____

_____

Do you believe you are responsible for the outcomes/results you get when you begin something? Or do you think your success is contingent on external circumstances? Explain.

_____

_____

_____

Are you are hard worker?   Yes_____   No_____

Do you believe attitudes/energy is "contagious," whether it's positive or negative?
Yes_____ No_____

If yes, describe a time when you felt as though you were "feeding" off another person's energy or attitude.

_____

_____

_____

_____

Do you believe in the concept that asserts, "What you focus on expands"? That is, when you dwell on something, it tends to happen (good or bad). For example, you obsess that the kids in the neighborhood will target your car on mischief night. You worry, wonder, and wait with anxiety. And... they do. Your car, in fact, is the only car they hit. This exact scenario happened to a housemate of mine many years ago. Or, you keep thinking about a friend you want to talk to, and suddenly, the phone rings; it's your friend calling.
Yes_____ No_____

If yes, note an occasion when this happened.

_____

_____

_____

_____

Do you believe there is a direct relationship between what you think (and say to yourself) and what you do?

Yes_____   No_____

Tell me about advice you often give out but rarely follow yourself.

_____

_____

_____

Do you want to be happy? Yes_____   No_____
If no, I don't think it's worth your while to continue because I'm eager to move you into the happiness and satisfaction that comes along with knowing yourself, liking yourself, and pursing things that engender self-respect, pride, pleasure, and a sense of personal achievement. I believe happiness is something we can choose.

How willing are you to express your true self by embracing the core values, talents, and personal goals that matter to you?

Extremely willing_____ willing_____ apprehensive_____ not willing yet____

Tell me a little more about your feelings as they relate to your willingness to move forward.

_____

_____

_____

Are you willing to commit time and energy toward securing your sense of self through the model of personal achievement?

Absolutely_____ I think so_____ Probably_____ Maybe_____

Did I ask too many questions? Yes____ No_____

Have any of these questions made you uncomfortable, or was any one too difficult to answer?
Yes____ No____
If yes, which one(s)? Explain why.

_____

_____

_____

_____

PART 2
Your *Values*

o o o o o o o o o o o o o o o o o o o o o o o o o o o o

"The greatest thing in the world is to know how to be one's own self."

—*Montaigne*

To be one's own self. Doesn't that sound easy and wonderful? To know *how* to be one's own self seems a bit more complicated. I think to start this process, you need to figure out who you are (what we just covered in Part 1), what's meaningful in your life (Part 2), and then act in accordance—congruent—with those core values (which we'll tackle in Part 3). Sounds easy enough, right? Well, I don't think easy, but I do think it's a fantastic way to approach life and find a sense of peace and happiness. So, this section is devoted to helping you discover the core values that guide your life. I've found that over time, with the busy schedule of families, and all the pulls and pushes of mom's time and energy, mom tends to overlook, forget, disregard, or sacrifice many of her deepest core values; the values that would otherwise help keep her feeling grounded, whole, and happy. I believe this is true because when I was interviewing moms for my book, I asked many questions related to needs, wants, preferences, dreams, goals, talents, etc. and few moms answered with any certainty.

Most moms turned and twisted in their seats, looked away in deep thought (although rarely answered), or asked me to "come back to that question."

In my own life, I have struggled to understand *how* to be my own self. What does that look like? What does that feel like? Is this about the clothes I wear, or the movies I watch, or the friends I have, or maybe the career path I chose? Since becoming a mom, I know for sure that I let go of my "self," and in doing so, I stumbled into bad space only to realize that I had to redefine myself in order to be my own self again. I started the journey back with identifying what was important to me; what gave significant meaning to my life. The one word that struck me like a lightning bolt was "creativity." That was missing, that was a big piece of my "self," and I was near desperate to have it back in my life. The wheels were put in motion that day as I wrestled with the details of how to put into place the very thing(s) that would help me live fully into the "how" of being me.

A core value is an aspect of your life that incites a strong, visceral reaction in your gut; a reaction so strong that there's no doubt your life is enhanced in some way by incorporating this value. A core value provides meaning in your world; it's an esteemed element of your life and shapes you to a large degree. Many things have meaning in my life. I esteem family, education, and fitness to name a few; I value honesty, humor, and the quiet pockets of my day, and my mind, where solitude prevails and rejuvenates my spirit. Over the years I have neglected many of the things I value because of circumstances, the same circumstances that led me *toward* activities and roles I didn't value. For instance, I've never been much of a chef. In fact, I can almost say that I hate the kitchen. Okay. I hate cooking, not the kitchen. Yet, as a mom of three young children, I spent nearly 80- 90% of my time in and around the kitchen, cooking and cleaning. Not a core value!

However, I eventually found myself through a variety of "tools" and the willingness to push myself over the obstacles that I knew would constantly be there to hurdle. I began by listing as many values that meant something to me. Then I narrowed the list down to my top ten core values and focused on making sure they were "nurtured" or "exercised" in some way, every day. It's okay to take baby steps, as long as you're constantly moving in the right direction. Your core values are a guide (your roadmap) to finding your way to the feeling of congruency—I think a wonderful destination. **When you're congruent, and embracing your core values, who you are aligns with what you do and say, and how you act and feel. If you're saying, and feeling, and doing things that are not you—you know. You know something is wrong, and you're probably not happy (at the deepest level), even if the things that bring you the greatest joy (e.g., your children/spouse) fill your life.**

Knowing what gives meaning to your life, what adds color and dimension to *you*, warrants time and work. You have to put aside the time and do the work, which may include talking with a therapist, a coach, or joining a group committed to this process. It also includes time to sit still, and to simply think, uninterrupted. It seems that if mothers spend time sitting still, if they center their thoughts around themselves, even if for a short time, they often think of that as "wasting time." I know I did. I remember daydreaming about writing *Missing In Action*, and what topics I would cover if I ever got serious about writing it. Inevitably, I would jolt from my reverie with guilt, and my thoughts would swiftly shift to the more immediate task that I had just set aside. "What am I doing?" I would say to myself. "I've got to get this laundry started before the baby wakes up." Of course I did. Don't you know laundry is far more important than "wasting time" on your dreams, talents, goals, and ambitions?! Wow. When phrased that way, need I say more?

Unfortunately, I've heard the expression "wasting time" from enough mothers to believe that they don't acknowledge the core values that add *true* meaning and satisfaction to their lives. They grow accustom to thinking that (and behaving as though) meaning and satisfaction are derived from food shopping, keeping a clean house, getting all the homework done, staying on top of their children's extracurricular commitments, and ensuring that their children achieve "success" because others can witness these activities and judge them. If we complete these tasks without stumbling, we are satisfied. And we find meaning in being the "good mommy." However, I want to go beyond this baseline sense of satisfaction and meaning for one great reason. In finding the core values that add meaning at the deepest level of our being, we fill the proverbial well. And we, as women and mothers, must fill that well daily, consistently, if we want to be happy and healthy. Just as a diabetic must maintain an ideal level of blood sugar to feel his or her best physically, emotionally, and mentally, mothers must keep their level of self-care at an ideal level or they will "crash." Mothers *must* rely on good habits if the goal is to live a good life, and feel as though they are congruent and comfortable in their own skin, living out their most esteemed values and achieving personal ambitions that will lift them up and sustain them through the tedious and challenging task of raising their children.

Simply put, when the well is full, you are more likely to feel strong, energetic, optimistic, and full of spirit. You will feel more of what you are naturally, unencumbered by the layers of obligations, responsibilities, and chores that can otherwise bury you. When the well is empty, you will fall prey to MIA and all the symptoms associated with it, including the eventual feeling of despair if that well never gets filled. But before we start thinking about what will fill that well, I want you to rate on a scale of 0 – 10, how you perceive these areas of your life, with 0 being "really bad/very unsatisfying" and 10 being "great/very satisfying."

Rate from 0 - 10

Relationship with your significant other _____

Relationship with your child(ren) _____

Physical health _____

Emotional well-being ____

Friendships ____

Financial status/money ____

Sex life ____

Career ____

Self-care ____

Spirituality ____

Creativity ____

Sense of independence ____

Personal ambitions ____

Intellectual stimulation ____

Social outlets/adult gatherings ____

Fun/recreation ____

This rating system gives you a quick glance at your life. It shows you what areas you might want to focus on (bringing you closer to a 10) and what areas may not matter so much to you. It's good information to have as we move along.

Next, you'll see a list of some core values. Pick six from the following values (or generate some of your own) that are most meaningful to you. Highlight them with a marker or put an asterisk next to them.

independence	resourcefulness	intimacy
commitment	beauty	nature
honesty	success	change
adventure	privacy	challenge
intelligence	perseverance	problem-solving
humor	mastery	service
friendship	cleanliness	justice
simplicity	innovation	pleasure
challenge	improvement	peace
vitality	time	power
faith	dedication	fame
creativity	loyalty	competition
excellence	solitude	progress
security	love	respect
money	health	style/flair
simplicity	knowledge	affection
fun	courage	self-respect
initiative	synergy	education
integrity	self-awareness	inner harmony
work	discipline	discipline
playfulness	choice	personal- growth
organization	positive attitude	travel

Once you choose six values, I want you to think about what it is *specifically* that made you choose these values. What meaning do you give each word? That is, *how do you know* that these values are important to you? And perhaps, more importantly, how do you know when you are fulfilling these values in your life?

Describe what you are doing when you're satisfying one of these core values.

_____

_____

_____

When ideally aligned with a core value, what do you see, hear, and/or feel?   In other words, how do you know it's being actualized?

_____

_____

_____

_____

How do you know when a core value is *not* being fulfilled?   Describe what you might see, hear, or feel.

_____

_____

_____

_____

Every value listed above is measurable in some way; that is, by the way someone is treating you differently, by the way you feel inside, by a tangible asset, by the behavior you're exhibiting, by the results you're achieving, etc.   It may be difficult to measure, or incorporate, some values in your life given your daily circumstances. For example, as much as you may want "financial independence," a sick baby or a personal injury/ disability (e.g., Multiple Sclerosis) may prevent you from working and maintaining your own income streams. This scenario would leave you unable to incorporate the core value of financial independence as you formerly defined it. It may require a new definition or the need to focus on other values more compatible with your life circumstances. Other times, your core values may directly conflict with the core values of another family member, which could compromise your efforts to firmly establish them. In other words, there could be a conflict of interest between you and your spouse. Life circumstances, timing, and other family members may affect how, when, and to what degree we integrate core values.

Are there life circumstances that do (or could) interfere with your ability to incorporate the core values you seek to embrace?

Yes_____ No_____

If yes, explain.

_____

_____

_____

_____

Is your significant other willing and able to support your efforts to secure the core values central to your personal happiness and well-being?

Yes_____ No_____

If No, explain.

_____

_____

_____

_____

Explain any challenge you believe could interfere with your desire to feel better, be happier, and become all that you aspire to be.

_____

_____

_____

_____

_____

The questions below were originally designed for my book *Missing In Action* and for use during workshops I facilitate. These are some of my favorite questions because they really work to exhume the self that often gets buried under the tasks related to our lives as mothers. The answers should be stated as simply as possible so I only gave you two lines in which to write. Also, I intentionally asked similar questions to weed out what may have been forgotten over time. Try not to overanalyze or overthink. Answer from your gut, as visceral responses are very telling. You always have the opportunity to go back and change or add something.

What do you like most about yourself?

_____

_____

How would you most like to feel?

_____

_____

Who makes you feel good about yourself and why?

_____

_____

What personal affront makes you most angry?

_____

_____

What do you admire most about yourself?

_____

_____

What do you feel most passionate about?

_____

_____

When you daydream, what do you see?

_____

_____

What's one thing you really want to do?

_____

_____

What's one thing you'd like to see happen?

_____

_____

What's one talent you possess?

_____

_____

What do you want to do most of all?

_____

_____

What's your favorite way to procrastinate?

_____

_____

What skill or talent would you love to possess?

_____

_____

What does your "child within" want to get or do?

_____

_____

What's one good thought that can distract you?

_____

_____

What's one impulse you'd like to act on?

_____

_____

What's one way you'd like to see yourself grow?

_____

_____

What do you do when you are all alone?

_____

_____

What would you do if you had more time?

_____

_____

What would you do if you had more money?

_____

_____

What do you wish you could create/build/design/learn?

_____

_____

What does your ideal day include?

_____

_____

What does your ideal "self" look like?

_____

_____

When you were young, what did you want to become?

_____

_____

If you were to give yourself one present, what would it be?

_____

_____

What activity causes you to forget time and the rest of the world?

_____

_____

What's one thing you yearn for?

_____

_____

What is your greatest strength?

_____

_____

What makes you feel resentful?

_____

_____

When do you feel most content?

_____

_____

What do you love to do so much that you would be willing to pay money to do it?

_____

_____

Now, go back and reread each question. Underline the key words in each answer or provide a single word that reflects that answer. For instance, if you answered the first question with a statement such as "I really like the fact that I can hear both sides of an argument without jumping to harsh conclusions," you would put in the margin a word like "fair-minded" or "nonjudgmental" or another word you think pinpoints your answer. If the answer is more like, "I work hard when I work but enjoy playing when I play," you can simply underline the key words. "I <u>work hard</u> when I work but enjoy <u>playing</u> when I play." By the time you get to the end of this particular exercise, you will have a string of words—definitely worth noting because they reflect some core values.

Isn't it interesting to see your core values come to life in your words? Are you seeing the same words popping up in this exercise as some of the core values you chose a few pages back (from the list)? Slowly but surely, you're seeing, feeling, and acknowledging what has great meaning in your life. However, *knowing* what has meaning is not enough. I want you to *own* those things that have great meaning in your life. In *Missing In Action*, I talk about why and how to create boundaries around your core values.   A boundary declares to yourself and others where a line must be drawn to safeguard you and what's important to you. A physical boundary may be as obvious as a fence, and a social boundary as subtle (and literal) as a step back and away from those who stand too close.

Likewise we can establish boundaries to declare at what point we feel manipulated, criticized, taken advantage of, or extended beyond reason. Boundaries act as a set of limits that preserve our personal identity, uniqueness, and autonomy; they safeguard those aspects of our lives that create an optimal degree of emotional, physical, psychological, mental, social, and spiritual well-being. In other words, boundaries protect us, our values, and the aspects of our selves that evidence in those values.

Next, go back and gather the words that have broken free from your idle thoughts and stream of consciousness; the words you underlined; the words with an asterisk next to them. Recognize that you embody many values that guide your life, consciously or not. Begin to acknowledge what values are in play consistently in your life, those that are not, and the ones you want to elevate to a higher order of priority.   And finally, with the complete understanding that I'm about to propose what could be a difficult task, I would like you to sit with the core values (the various words you highlighted and underlined) that meant the most to you. This could be two or three words—nine or ten. With these words, create a statement of self.

For instance, "I am (creative) and (athletic) because when I (write), (play tennis), and (work out), my energy levels soar and I feel happy. By being

(<u>creative and athletic</u>), I will become a more fulfilled, happier person and a better mom."

Jot down your statement of self.

_____

_____

_____

You don't have to use this sequencing or this particular sentence; I'm only offering this as an example. You can construct this statement of self however you like (whatever works for you) and *conclude with any positive outcome you want*.

From this statement of self, extract at least one way (i.e., one course of action) you can take to ensure that your positive outcome is achieved. This is called a goal.

State your goal here, as precisely and clearly as possible.

_____

_____

_____

Great Job!!

Congratulations. You've done a lot of good work so far. And now, you've got a great goal in mind, a goal that reflects *you* and at least one core value. The next step is to pursue this goal. The mere *act* of pursuing your goal will build your confidence and create greater self-esteem. There's nothing like working toward a personal goal to lift your spirits, energize you, and make you feel good about yourself. This feeling will spill over into every other area of your life, including your life as mom. You'll feel stronger, happier, and balanced in a way you've not felt before engaging your interests, talents, and goals.

PART 3
Your *Goals*

o o o o o o o o o o o o o o o o o o o o o o o o o o o o

"I know of no more encouraging fact than the unquestion-able ability of man [woman] to elevate his [her] life by conscious endeavor."

—*Henry David Thoreau*

"Whatever you can do, or believe you can do, begin it now. Genius has boldness, power, and magic in it. Begin it now!"

—*Goethe*

At different points in life, we can, and often do, lose sight and release from our grip the very things that make us who we are. This is human, and understandable, especially for moms because we are often pulled in all kinds of directions and have the pressure from society to be the "caregiver" to those who need us (e.g., children, spouse, charitable causes, aging parents). But this is exactly why we *must* provide the self-care that *works*!

From this day forward, I want you to see your potential and your capacity to lead the most satisfying life you could lead. I want you to believe you can pursue your talents, interests, ambitions, and goals despite the obstacles that consistently seek to sabotage your efforts. I want you to listen to your inner voice (the positive self-talk!) because it's your guide when you veer off the road. You answered the hard questions in Part 1 and Part 2, and so, you know who you are and what matters to you even if you temporarily lose your way.

I do offer this bit of advice, though, before we delve into your goals and how to achieve them: Say the "no" you learned to say through appropriate boundary setting (if you read *Missing In Action*). Tune out those who are not encouraging. If you can, avoid people (friends, family) who are negative. Walk away from negative encounters and stressful situations. These will drain you and make it all the harder to keep moving toward the most effective self-care you can provide for yourself. You need to surround yourself with positive people, happy people, and people who understand and support what you want to achieve. This will go a long way in helping you accomplish your goal(s).

~~~~~~~~~~~~~~~~

At the end of the last section, I asked you to describe one way that would lead you to fulfill the statement of self that you constructed. This is your goal, and as you know, I believe wholeheartedly that having a personal goal that reflects *your* interests, needs, or ambitions (vs. goals associated with your family/children) is the greatest step you can take toward your self-care. And, by taking care of yourself, you will find that you have more to give others, especially your family and friends. You'll have more energy, interest, and patience than ever before. You'll be happier, more confident, and secure. Personal goals are a wonderful thing. ☺

Now, let's work at making your goal as specific as possible. The more specific you make your goal, the clearer you become on what it is you really want and how to go about getting it.

Rewrite your goal. For example, "I want to start painting again."

_____

_____

_____

Why do you want it? It's critical to know the *why* to what you're doing. For example, painting satisfies your creative self and is an outlet for daily frustrations. Or, losing weight will make you look and feel better about yourself.

_____

_____

_____

What about (the result) is important to you? In other words, I'm asking you to go a step deeper into the 'why' of what you want. For instance, you want to work outside the home because you want to earn extra money for yourself and your family. That's a wonderful goal. So, extra money is important to you. Why? What does extra money provide/do for you? Include literal and psychological benefits. That is, extra money is important to you because...

_____

_____

_____

Does your goal align with any one of your core values? Which one? Explain.

_____

_____

_____

_____

When considering your goal, ask yourself the following questions, if applicable.
When, where, how often, and with whom.

With the example above, regarding a job, you might ask yourself: Where do I want to work (what industry, with what population, etc.)? When do I want to work (beginning in January or when Johnnie starts kindergarten, etc.)? How often do I want to work (three days a week, all week, just mornings, or only weekends)? With whom do I want to work (private sector, corporate, with my husband/best friend, or by myself)?

When:_____

_____

Where:_____

_____

How often:_____

_____

With whom:_____

_____

_____

How do you imagine your outcome? In other words, how will you know when you've gotten what you want? What will you see, hear, feel, touch, or taste? Be very specific here. You'll be testing your outcome against this answer someday. Besides, you want to know when you've "arrived." Anything short of this, and you're not quite done.

_____

_____

_____

_____

Is your frame of reference internal (you) or external (others)? That is, when you think you've reached your goal, do you know because of what you feel/see/hear or how others receive/perceive you or respond to you? Check one. Then, circle the one that's more important to you. These could be different.

Internal_____   External_____

What would you give up in order to get what you want? Most goals come with a price tag. There'll be sacrifices to make along the way. Know this now, and be clear about what you're willing to do/give up and what you're not willing to do/give up. The answer might include things such as luxuries, family time, or friends that don't support you. This could be a temporary situation until you've achieved your goal.

_____

_____

_____

When you get what you want, what else in your life will improve?

_____

_____

_____

_____

How does NOT getting what you want serve you or benefit you? For instance, take the example of wanting a job. You may have to give up time with your children. In answering this question, then, by *not* getting what you want, you would still be home/available for your children—and perhaps not missing out on all those special moments. Likewise, if you don't get a job, you avoid any feelings of guilt that may have surfaced if you had secured a job outside the home. Can you see where I'm going with this? This question is very important and serves to look at unconscious/subconscious motivating factors that could hinder your efforts to achieve a goal. So, take your time on this question, and discuss it with a friend/spouse for additional feedback since the answer might evade you (I did say they're unconscious/subconscious factors!)

_____

_____

_____

_____

_____

_____

What would happen if you do not achieve your outcome/goal? This is not quite the same question as the last. As per the wanting to get a job example of a goal, you might feel that in not getting a job and earning extra money, you may have to remain a stay-at-home mom longer than you had hoped or planned.

_____

_____

_____

_____

What resources do you have available to help you achieve your stated goal? That is, people, places, money, opportunities, etc.

_____

_____

_____

_____

How can you best utilize the resources you have available?

_____

_____

_____

_____

What would stop you from accessing the above resources and/or stop you from pursuing your goal? For instance, some women feel self-conscious about asking for help. Or maybe you're afraid of failing or afraid you'll upset someone by not being as available.

_____

_____

_____

_____

By when do you want to achieve this goal and see/hear/feel your specific outcome? Determine a deadline.

_____

_____

What are you going to do right NOW to get what you want?

_____

_____

_____

_____

Finally, complete the sentence below, including the relevant information from above. For example, "I want a new job outside the home as soon as Johnnie starts pre-school. I want to work three days a week, 9 – 5, at a marketing firm within a 20 mile radius from home. This job will utilize my skills and experience and provide an extra $___ a month for me and my family to do (_____) while giving me more knowledge and the confidence to start my own marketing company in the next five years." Yes, you can always include a bigger goal. See if you can formulate a more precise version of your original goal.

I want

_____

_____

_____

_____

A "good" goal is achievable and measurable, and by measurable I mean you can see, feel, and describe a difference. For example, if alone time is valuable in your life as it is in mine, you'll be able to say that you've acquired alone time because between 2 and 3 o'clock every day you have a babysitter or mommy's helper at the house to take care of your kids. Being alone for an hour is measurable. If you picked "nature" as a value, you can attest to the fact that you went hiking in the past week or planted some flowers in your backyard. Even a vague goal, such as "I want to become more spiritual" can convert into a more tangible goal by asking the right questions. For instance, "What would 'become more spiritual' look like, feel like, or sound like?" From those answers, you could extract a goal (e.g., attend a daily morning mass or fill my house with incense when mediating every Wednesday and Friday morning between 10 – 11). See what I mean?

Good goals also need to be challenging, believable, and clearly written in specific terms. We already fulfilled the last requirement in Part 3 of this workbook. Only you can determine if your goal is challenging and believable. Because you're a mom, I'm betting any goal will be challenging! However, my hope is that you define a goal that does challenge you to become more—more whole, more congruent, more vibrant, more energized, more centered, etc. And, as for believable, can *you* believe in your goal? Is it achievable? For instance, I have clients who use positive affirmations every day. However, those affirmations must be believable to work. You can't say, "I'm confident and happy" if you're not confident and happy. Your mind knows better, and because the affirmation is not believable to you, it's not likely to work. Rather, I advise my clients to say, "I'm *learning* to be confident and happy." This way, the affirmation *is* believable, and works!

Finally, I think it's important that your goal has a deadline. Perhaps in theory, a deadline isn't essential. Some people work on a goal their entire lives (e.g., spiritual awakening). However, with our objective in mind (i.e., your self-care), I prefer we set goals that have deadlines. Enroll in a dance class by_____. Lose 10 lbs. by_____. Finish graduate school by_____.

I want you to experience success and the feelings associated with achievement. I'd rather see you set a deadline and have to push it back than not setting a deadline at all. A deadline is a great motivating force, especially if there's a consequence or reward attached to it. I had a client who set a goal to find a son she gave up for adoption many years ago. She felt strongly about this goal and the need to soothe the ache within her. It was hard to affix a deadline to this goal, but coincidentally, when a family reunion was set, she concentrated her efforts, spent a little money, and strengthened her determination. She arrived at the family reunion with her son by her side! It's amazing what we can do when we combine passion, determination, and a great incentive.

I'm hoping through this workbook you found your passion so that you can pursue it with unyielding determination, which will lift you to greater heights physically, emotionally, mentally, financially, spiritually, and/or psychologically. If that's not enough incentive for you, think what a happier, healthier mom will be like for your children and spouse. It'll make a world a difference, trust me. I know firsthand the difference I feel, see, and hear when I'm overwhelmed and lost in motherhood vs. what I feel, see, and hear when I'm pursuing my personal ambitions. So, take the first step (which tends to be the hardest) and set your goal in motion.

Below I offer my personal set of principles, the principles that guided me toward the achievement of my goals—the principles I believe can propel people toward success.

Principles of Success
- Definition
- Desire
- Decision
- Discipline
- Determination
- Deadline
- Declaration

Genuine beginnings begin within us, even when they are brought to our attention by external opportunities—William Bridges

The capacity to **Define** a goal relies on clarity. You must state in positive language what you wish to add to your life, not what you should avoid. Clearly articulate what it is *exactly* that you want and how you can achieve your goal. The more specific you can be in your definition of the goal, the better—for your sake as well as for others. The definition is complete when it includes an *organized plan of action*; the how to get what you want. In using specific words to describe your goal and how you plan to attain it, you leave no room for wonder or doubt. Choose words that indicate what you will see, hear, taste, or feel in your acquisition of the goal. These words make it real and enticing.

In my experience, definition leads naturally to **Desire**. When describing something you want, you whet your appetite for it. The image of it, the vision of you cultivating a garden, for instance, or creating a beautiful watercolor, will likely provoke an urgency in you to begin planting or painting. At least that's how it happened for me. I saw myself writing in a quiet room facing an inspiring ocean. The more I envisioned it, the more I wanted it. My desire grew until I could not *not* write. In other words, I HAD to write. The desire to write outweighed the less meaningful activities that called me. I continued to clean the house, change diapers, and vacuum, but I also created my room for writing. The room didn't face the ocean, but it was quiet. In fact, it was the very room where my husband had once found me crying about being MIA (the infamous attic story).

The ability to **Decide** is harder than it may look. We all have tendencies to be indecisive; to procrastinate. But make a decision you must. You are either in, or not. I decided it was time to write. And I wrote. You need to decide if your goal is feasible at this time in your life and then assess whether or not the goal "works" with the other members of your family. If your goal impedes, or is perceived as threatening to, the well-being of another family member, the goal will not be well-received and might be under constant "attack." This is the aspect of decision making that is difficult. Therefore, I recommend that you anticipate and explain the ancillary effects of your goal on all members of the family and ensure the positive nature of the goal on *everyone* (e.g., your better mood makes you a more patient parent). Once this ecological balance is established, discipline is necessary to move a goal along in the right direction.

Discipline, like all the other tenets, is an absolute must. I completed my *Missing In Action* manuscript over many missed holidays with the extended family and day trips with my husband and kids. Although for some mothers reading this workbook, a quiet weekend devoted to writing (and not caregiving) sounds joyful; it wasn't. In the beginning it was a great respite, but over time it demanded discipline in large order. I had a demanding task before me, the desire to do it, and the self-control to sit long hours at a computer on many sunny and perfectly mild days. Discipline is the character you need to befriend. Without discipline, you cannot move toward and accomplish any goal of merit. I consider it my lynch pin; pull it out and everything crumbles.

Determination is the visceral piece of your quest. It resides not only in your mind but in your gut as well. When someone or something threatens your goal, it's your determination that rears its "fixed" head and sets the stance for battle. Knowing mothers as I do, they rarely fall short of determination when they make up their minds to do something. Unfortunately, however, they rarely demonstrate this resolve when it relates to ensuring one of their *own* needs or desires (or their self-care). Perhaps this is because the goal was never completely defined, the desire was never fully aroused, or the decision was never firmly made. Maybe they never thought about themselves long enough to design the plan of action or exercise the tenacity that drives their ideas. All said, once a goal is alive, determination keeps it breathing. I established my goal not only to write, but to write *Missing In Action* (and this workbook, and ebooks, etc.). Many things from obligations to guilt caused me to pause, but it was my determination that brought me back to the computer.

Setting a **Deadline** gave me a sense of accountability. I had no boss breathing down my neck, no friend waiting at the gym, no flowers that would die if I didn't start planting. A deadline gave me a date in which to start *and* to finish. Without it, I was certain to dawdle. And last on this daunting list of principles is the capacity to **Declare** your intentions. In no uncertain terms, write out each piece of the Principles of Success listed above in *your* words, with *your* core values and goals at the center of *your* thoughts. Leave nothing out, for each piece is essential to the attainment of all your goals—the goals that incorporate the core values that provide peace, vitality, and sustenance for your sense of self. Read it aloud every day to convince yourself that in declaring your goals, you influence your own subconscious mind to succeed, which in turn, guarantees success as *you* define it. In the very best way, I resumed a life colored by the many shades of me. I redirected my life with each decision I made and every action I took, which led me closer to the sense of self I aspired to reclaim.

Not an easy progression toward goal achievement, to say the least. Most people cannot adequately define what they want, stir and maintain desire, firmly decide to pursue a goal, implement the discipline, remain determined, adhere to a deadline, and relentlessly declare their objective until they succeed. Yet, these are the principles that I truly believe were key to my success. You should know that often I neglected to apply these principles, and often I failed to accomplish my goals. However, I always got back on track. I believe that all seven principles must be applied in order for our most ambitious goals to be realized. I also appreciate how difficult it is for busy mothers to apply these principles on a daily basis. So I advise mothers, especially new mothers, to take small steps and build on their minor accomplishments. The journey toward goal achievement is, in itself, energizing. Eventually, with perseverance, you may see that you're integrating these principles, or your own formula, into the script you need to realize your core values, and embed those values into goals that support your true self and greatest ambitions.

Through this workbook, and with concentrated effort, attention, and commitment, you have already defined what you want in very specific terms so that you, your family, the community at IMC, and the universe can hear you! So scratch off Definition and Declaration. I also asked you to set a deadline a few pages back, so that piece is done. The rest is up to you. Decide—to pursue your interest, talent, or goal. Decide to be disciplined, and determined. Decide—to consider your self-care a priority. Decide—to feel your best and let that feeling generate a better life for you and your family. You've come this far. Keep going.

At InMomsCorner.com, you'll find camaraderie and accountability. Few people have known success without accountability. At InMomsCorner. com, you can access the tools (e.g., chats, ebooks, workshops, coaching) that will help you find your "self," maintain strong boundaries, and create the positive self-talk that generates success and greater well-being. At InMomsCorner.com, we're sisters on a journey and committed to the ultimate form of self-care: Personalized self-care—through the values and goals that make each of us unique, centered, and true to ourselves.

Sure, there will be obstacles along the way, always. There can be physical obstacles, such as illness, or psychological obstacles, such as anxiety or depression. People generally battle information overload and become paralyzed. Or they lack information and become discouraged. And then, there are people who procrastinate or lack discipline, time management skills, money, or adequate support from others. For most, it's easier to walk away from a worthy goal than to persevere day after day. Unfortunately, as you might know, data shows that most of us quit just inches before success greets us. This one thought sustained me through my toughest days. I would think, "How close am I?" I guess I always thought I *was* just inches away, even though that wasn't always true.

What obstacles do you anticipate? Be honest, whether it's your lack of discipline or another's lack of support; money; time constraints, etc.

_____

_____

Write down as many possible ways to overcome these obstacles.
(e.g., a babysitter, a loan, a continuing education class)

_____

_____

And remember for the sake of your self-care and well-being, *pursuing* an interest, talent, or goal has just as much power as achieving it. Well, I know that achieving your goal would feel fabulous, but the point I'm trying to make is that the journey matters. The journey toward goal achievement is full of great energy, and great people, and wonderful moments that build you up and strengthen your sense of self. So despite occasional setbacks or feelings of discouragement, take a step every day, seek to overcome the obstacles that present. Do one thing that inches you closer to your goal! Recognize the partial accomplishments you're making and the positive impact these accomplishments are having on you. This goal is important to you, obviously, or you wouldn't be here. So, remember to breathe, push forward, and feel your "self" filling up with the kind of energy your body, mind, and spirit need to thrive.

And last, but not least, remember that you make choices around what you're going to do and what you're not going to do, even if you don't verbalize or consciously recognize that you're choosing. Be intentional. Choose well.

ADDITIONAL TIPS FOR ACHIEVING YOUR GOAL

- Listen to upbeat, inspiring music, seminars, and people to get your juices flowing. This has *always* worked for me.

- It helps to have on-going smaller (short-term) goals that support the larger goal. By accomplishing the smaller goals, one by one, you gain confidence as you seek to achieve your bigger goal.

- Strive for balance. Your life is full, and you have many areas of your life to consider, including your health, relationships, finances, career, and children.

- Being divided and pulled in all directions can cause you to lose focus on your goals. Recognize this and get back on track as soon as possible.

- Wake up every morning and ask yourself, "What will I focus on today?" And by the way, you don't have to pursue a task related to your goal every day if that becomes too difficult. Decide what's more reasonable and doable, and do that. You will reach your goal all the same even if you designate certain days of the week to pursue your goal. Some moms simply cannot put aside time every day to satisfy a personal need, want, interest, or ambition.

- Stay tuned into your resources of time, money, energy, patience, etc. as you pursue your goal. Typically there are limits to such resources. You may have to get creative and think "outside the box" if any of these resources become unavailable.

- Recognize and celebrate partial accomplishments.

- Adjust a deadline if necessary without being critical of yourself. You'll get there as long as you persevere and stay committed to your well-being.

- If your goal is dependent on another person, such as "I want to start a business with Tom," recognize that although the outcome is influenced by your efforts/actions, it is not completely in your control. You can't always make someone adhere to your timetables and objectives or devote the same amount of energy and time as you. Keep a more flexible frame of mind under these conditions.

In Mom's Corner
Be there, for yourself.

Please join us at InMomsCorner.com where we share our lives and move courageously toward doing for ourselves in ways that make us feel energized, balanced, confident, and happy at our core...because when we feel good, everyone wins!